The *Grace* *of* *Gratitude*

The Grace of Gratitude

PAUL MALLARD

10 Publishing

First published in Great Britain in 2021

British Library Cataloguing in Publication Data
A record for this book is available from the British Library

ISBN: 978-1-913896-08-9

Designed and typeset by Pete Barnsley (CreativeHoot.com)

Printed in the UK

10Publishing, a division of 10ofthose.com
Unit C, Tomlinson Road, Leyland, PR25 2DY, England

Email: info@10ofthose.com
Website: www.10ofthose.com

1 3 5 7 10 8 6 4 2

Contents

Choosing gratitude

A study in contrasts

I spent the summer before going to university helping an elderly lady who occasionally came to our church. I would cut her lawn and do minor jobs around the garden. Each time I had finished, she would serve lemonade and tell me her life story. She must have been so lonely – though I was too young and naïve to feel her pain. Her story, oft-repeated, was a tragic one. She had fallen in love as a young woman, but her father had forbidden the relationship and so it had ended. This affected her health – she became ill with rheumatic fever. It also tied her to the parental home so that her mature years had been spent caring for aging parents. She always ended with the same diatribe: 'My father ruined my life. I nursed him, but I can never forgive him. I'm still angry when I think about it.'

Anger had congealed into bitterness that became the background music of her life. She was kind to me, but her experience had strangled and destroyed her life. I don't know whether she ever became a Christian and found the release that forgiveness brings, but her story is a warning about the danger of bitterness. She died alone during my first term at university.

During that first term I became friends with Andy, a third-year law student. I was a working-class lad with a strong Brummie accent; Andy was an old Etonian with an elegant turn of phrase. The gospel really does break down barriers!

Andy suffered from a progressive and aggressive muscular disease which severely limited his mobility. At the age of twenty-one he looked like an old man, leaning on a stick and struggling with stairs. He was in constant pain and knew that his life expectations were severely limited.

Yet he was one of the most joyful Christians I have ever met. His life was marked by gratitude and thankfulness in a way that was infectious. He was one of the strongest evidences of the power of grace that I have ever known. His life made Jesus visible, intelligible and desirable. He could have chosen the path of bitterness, but instead he chose the way of gratitude. It was a deliberate and daily decision to look beyond suffocating circumstances and to focus on God's goodness.

Two stories and two very different responses.

We all have our own stories. Sometimes the circumstances of life seem overwhelming. At such times we face a choice. We can become resentful, angry and bitter. Or we can look beyond the trial to the gracious faithfulness of God and respond in thankfulness and gratitude.

We cannot control our circumstances, but we can control our response. Gratitude is a choice. And it is a choice which bears succulent and sustaining fruit.

Reasons to be grateful

Gratitude appreciates the good things that God has poured into our lives. More than that, it deliberately affirms the goodness and worth of the Giver. Secular writers acknowledge that gratitude fosters psychological and physical health. Studies have shown that a negative mindset can lead to bitterness, resentment and anger, and can easily spiral into depression.

This should not surprise us, since it is just what the Bible teaches. What is less clear is how a secular world view, which leaves God entirely out of the picture, can ever foster a gratitude which is immune to the adverse circumstances of life. The beauty of the Christian faith is that our gratitude is focused on the God who is above our situation and whose plans are always for our ultimate good. Like Habakkuk we can declare,

> *Though the fig-tree does not bud*
> *and there are no grapes on the vines,*
> *though the olive crop fails*
> *and the fields produce no food,*
> *though there are no sheep in the sheepfold*
> *and no cattle in the stalls,*
> *yet I will rejoice in the LORD,*
> *I will be joyful in God my Saviour.*

*The Sovereign L*ORD *is my strength;*
  he makes my feet like the feet of a deer,
  he enables me to tread on the heights.

(Habakkuk 3:17–19)

The Assyrian came down

To help us explore the grace of gratitude we will focus on Psalm 66 in the subsequent chapters of this book.

This is an anonymous psalm of thanksgiving written to celebrate a great national deliverance. Many commentators link it to the defeat of the Assyrian army before the gates of Jerusalem, which is recorded in 2 Kings 19. The Assyrians were the undefeated superpower of the day. They had already conquered Israel and captured Samaria (2 Kings 17). Now they had a stranglehold on Jerusalem. In the words of the poet Byron,

The Assyrian came down like the wolf
  on the fold,
And his cohorts were gleaming in purple
  and gold;

And the sheen of their spears was like stars
   on the sea,
When the blue wave rolls nightly on
   deep Galilee.[1]

Godly King Hezekiah prayed and the Lord delivered his people:

That night the angel of the LORD went out and put to death a hundred and eighty-five thousand in the Assyrian camp. When the people got up the next morning – there were all the dead bodies! So, Sennacherib king of Assyria broke camp and withdrew. He returned to Nineveh and stayed there (2 Kings 19:35–36).

Byron immortalises it in the conclusion of his poem:

And the widows of Ashur are loud in their wail,
And the idols are broke in the temple of Baal;

---

[1] Lord Byron first published 'The Destruction of Sennacherib' in 1815 in his *Hebrew Melodies*.

And the might of the Gentile, unsmote by
the sword,
Hath melted like snow in the glance of
the Lord!

Just a glance from God scatters his enemies and saves his people.

We cannot be dogmatic, but Psalm 66 would certainly fit in with this great display of God's saving power. The psalm reflects on the history of God's people and is realistic about the ups and downs of their experience. At the same time, however, it is bubbling over with thankfulness and will help us to engage with this subject ourselves.

Reflections

1. Why is bitterness dangerous?

2. How can we be grateful in spite of our circumstances?

3. Read the story of the deliverance of Jerusalem in 2 Kings 19:1–37. What does it teach about prayer and about God?

The call to gratitude

The missing jewel

One Sunday morning, as she sat in church, my wife discovered that she had lost the diamond from her engagement ring. We searched carefully, but to no effect. The diamond was lost. My wife was distraught. I gave her the ring when I proposed to her over forty years ago. Its personal value was much greater than its monetary worth.

As soon as we got home, I made a fingertip search of the kitchen and there, sparkling in the corner, was the diamond. It is now firmly reattached to its original setting!

In 1961 A.W. Tozer described worship as *'the missing jewel in the evangelical church'*. However strong we may be in other spiritual areas, a neglect of worship will impoverish our church and our Christian experience.[2]

It would have been an act of crass insensitivity to tell my wife not to worry about her lost diamond. Yet we sometimes undervalue the importance of public worship. If the preaching is right, isn't that all that matters at church? Don't we just want to get through the 'preliminaries', such as the singing, so that we can get to the sermon?

According to Romans 12:1–2, worship involves the daily dedication of our lives to God, which we offer up to him in a grateful response to his abundant grace. Public worship is no substitute for practical devotion. However, this does not negate the importance of the worship which we offer when we meet our fellow believers to delight in God's worth, declare his glory and confess his greatness. Such worship is the response of all that I am to all that God has revealed of himself in Christ.

---

[2] A.W. Tozer's sermon was expanded to a short book: *Worship Missing Jewel Evangelism* (Christian Publications, 1992).

Worship flows from a grateful heart. We can see this in Psalm 66.

Shout and sing and say

Psalm 66 begins with three invitations to draw near to God in thankful praise:

> *Shout for joy to God, all the earth!*
> *Sing the glory of his name;*
> *make his praise glorious.*
> *Say to God, 'How awesome are your deeds!*
> *So great is your power*
> *that your enemies cringe before you.*
> *All the earth bows down to you;*
> *they sing praise to you,*
> *they sing the praises of your name.'*
>
> *(verses 1–4)*

The first invitation is to *'Shout for joy to God'* (verse 1).

Here is a call for loud, exuberant praise. Gratitude is not a refined recitation of appreciation – a muffled, polite mumble. It's a full-blooded and ear-splitting shout of praise. The same Hebrew word is used to describe the shout which accompanied the collapse of the walls of Jericho (Joshua 6:20).

Notice too that it is to be a joyful shout. This is where we often go wrong. Joy is a vital characteristic of all true Christianity – but it is not based on temperament or circumstances or emotion. We can have joy in our hearts even when we have tears in our eyes. Joy is a deep-seated delight which is grounded in the unchanging and unshakable character of God. Joy is not the absence of suffering; it is the presence of God. It is the fruit of the Spirit in the soul of man (Galatians 5:22).

The source of joy lies outside itself. If we pursue joy, we will lose joy; if we purse God, we will find it:

> *You make known to me the path of life;*
> *you will fill me with joy in your presence,*
> *with eternal pleasures at your right hand.*
> *(Psalm 16:11)*

A sharper focus

Secondly, we are to 'Sing the glory of his name' (Psalm 66:2).

The Bible contains at least fifty commands to sing and nearly five hundred references to singing. For Christians singing is not an optional extra. When you become a Christian, you become a singer. At creation *the morning stars sang together and all the angels shouted for joy'* (Job 38:7). There were songs at midnight when Jesus was born (Luke 2:13–14). Singing is one evidence of the fullness the Spirit (Ephesians 5:18–20), and heaven is a place of song (Revelation 4–5).

As we sing, we magnify God's name together (Psalm 34:3). What does this mean? Think of a telescope. It does not make celestial objects bigger, but it makes them clearer. That is what we do when we sing God's praises. Of course, we cannot make God greater than he already is, but he comes into sharper focus as we declare his majesty in melody.

Gratitude will express itself in song, and often listening to Christian songs will tune our hearts to God's grace and vitalise our gratitude. In particular we are to sing the *'glory of his name'*. To know God's name is to know him. The test of a good song is that it leads to a clearer vision of the magnificence of God's glory. Our singing is not merely incidental – as mentioned before, we are not to consider it a necessary preliminary to the sermon, which we view as the real purpose of our gathering for worship. Singing should come from the overflow of our hearts as we gaze on the glory of God and anticipate heaven.

I was once present at a large Christian convention which concluded with the celebration of communion. The last song had been sung and the benediction was still hanging in the air when a single voice from the congregation began to sing shakily, 'There is a Redeemer, Jesus God's own Son'.[3] Without musical accompaniment three thousand voices joined in and finished the song. The moment was electrifying. It felt as close to heaven as I have ever been. If you are worried about the fact that you cannot hold a tune now, don't despair. When we get to heaven, voices will be provided!

[3.] 'There Is a Redeemer' is a song by Keith Green, from his album *Songs for the Shepherd* (1982).

A much-misused word

The third and final command is to address God: *'Say to God, "How awesome are your deeds!"'* (Psalm 66:3).

There is a wonderful circularity about worship. God comes to us in his Word and speaks his truth into our lives. We come to him in prayer and song as we reflect back our gratitude for what he has revealed. In particular we are to speak of his awesome deeds and irresistible power.

Today the word 'awesome' has been overused and emptied of its significance. We declare we have had an 'awesome holiday' or watched an 'awesome movie' or even eaten an 'awesome pizza'! The word should refer to something which is breathtaking and overwhelming. We might argue that only the God of the Bible is truly and properly awesome. He is not a tame and pathetic little God who can be comfortably managed. His nature and character and deeds are overwhelming, and any true encounter with God will be marked by both joyful confidence and godly fear. Gratitude flows from our limited comprehension of the incomprehensible.

Listen to John Piper:

If you don't see the greatness of God then all the things that money can buy become very exciting. If you can't see the sun you will be impressed with a street light. If you've never felt thunder and lightning you'll be impressed with fireworks. And if you turn your back on the greatness and majesty of God you'll fall in love with a world of shadows and short-lived pleasures.[4]

Notice that the psalmist's desire is that the world would share his wonder. The purpose of mission is to bring people from every continent, nation and people-group into the enjoyment of the triune God. Its goal is universal gratitude.

When your heart is full of gratitude, worship God. When you heart feels numb, worship God. When crushing circumstances want to control all your attention, worship God. True

---

[4.] Taken from John Piper's sermon 'The Curse of Careless Worship' based on Malachi 1:6–14 (Desiring God Ministries, 1 November 1987).

worship leads to wonder, gratitude, hope and joy. True worship fixes our attention outside of ourselves and nourishes the grace of gratitude. As we worship, we discover that the joy of the Lord really is our strength (Nehemiah 8:10).

Reflections

1. How can we best prepare ourselves for public worship?

2. Choose two or three of your favourite hymns or songs and use them to meditate on the character of God. What do you find to be grateful for there?

3. Read Hebrews 10:19–25. What do these verses teach us about worship?

The foundation of gratitude

Looking for the black cat

As part of my undergraduate study in theology, I sat in on some philosophy lectures. I found ancient or medieval philosophy fascinating, but I struggled with modern philosophy. It seem to go around in ever-decreasing circles without ever getting anywhere. I shared my frustrations with one of my friends who was studying philosophy: 'I don't get it. I just cannot understand where it is going.'

'Don't worry about it,' he responded soothingly. 'No one understands it! It is like a blind man, in a dark room, looking for a black cat – that isn't there.'

Philosophy which begins with an atheistic world view cannot get very far in the pursuit of ultimate knowledge. There have always been great Christian minds which have engaged with truth and demonstrated the essential reasonableness of Christianity. However, as we move into the next section of Psalm 66, we discover that biblical faith is not founded on the speculations of human reason. The Bible is an account of what God has done:

> *Come and see what God has done,*
> *his awesome deeds for mankind!*
>
> *(Psalm 66:5)*

It does not begin with an argument for God's existence, but with an affirmation of his actions: *'In the beginning God created the heavens and the earth'* (Genesis 1:1).

As the story unfolds, the Bible describes a God who plans and speaks, who promises and delivers. He is not a spectator wringing his hands in pathetic frustration. He is the living

God who acts. On the day of Pentecost, Peter invited his hearers to come and see what God had done:

> *This man was handed over to you by God's deliberate plan and foreknowledge; and you, with the help of wicked men, put him to death by nailing him to the cross. But God raised him from the dead, freeing him from the agony of death, because it was impossible for death to keep its hold on him (Acts 2:23–24).*

The gospel is not a call for a reformation of life. It is an account of God's saving deeds. Faith is not a blind leap into the dark. It is based on history – it is confidence based on evidence. This means that our gratitude is not subject to the swirling waters of human speculation. It is firmly anchored on the rock of the saving deeds of the living God.

On the other side of the sea

After the call to gratitude (66:1–4), the psalmist begins to list some of the reasons why God is worthy of our trust and thanks, reminding us that our God is the living God who acts in history (verse 5).

Two aspects of this are described. Firstly, he is the God who saves:

> *He turned the sea into dry land,*
> > *they passed through the waters on foot –*
> > *come, let us rejoice in him.*

> *(verse 6)*

The psalmist takes us back to the great act of salvation which led to the birth of the nation of Israel. This living God rescued his people from slavery in Egypt and brought them safely across the River Jordan, into the Promised Land. The ten plagues proved Yahweh's superiority to the gods of Egypt and showed that he was serious about keeping his promises and rescuing his people:

> *The LORD said, 'I have indeed seen the misery of my people in Egypt. I have heard them crying out because of their slave drivers, and I am concerned about their suffering. So I have come down to rescue them from the hand of*

the Egyptians and to bring them up out of that
land into a good and spacious land, a land
flowing with milk and honey' (Exodus 3:7–8).

This ought to have been enough to confirm the
people in their confidence in God. But when
they came to the Red Sea, they were suddenly
faced with an impassable barrier before them
and the invincible Egyptian army behind them,
and they panicked. Blaming Moses for their
dilemma, they asked why he had brought them
there to die (Exodus 14:11–12). In response
Moses focused their attention on the God who
has already proved that he is able to rescue:

Moses answered the people, 'Do not be afraid.
Stand firm and you will see the deliverance the
Lord will bring you today. The Egyptians you
see today you will never see again. The Lord
will fight for you; you need only to be still'
(Exodus 14:13-14).

The sea parted, they walked through on foot
and their enemies were crushed in the flood
that followed.

If you had asked them their story on the other side of the sea, what would they have said? Perhaps:

We were helpless and doomed to die under the Egyptian lash. We cried out to God and he sent us a deliverer. We have been saved by the blood of a lamb and by the mighty resurrection power that took us through the waters of death. We are here because of God's grace alone and we are confident that he will never desert us but will bring us safely into the place he promised.

Does that sound strangely familiar? That is our story and it is a source of constant and unending gratitude. At the cross we were saved and our enemies – sin and death and Satan – were crushed under the feet of our great Redeemer.

The response of the Israelites is to sing the first great hymn recorded in Scripture (Exodus 15:1–18). It is a gloriously God-centred hymn which drips with wonder and gratitude to the God who saves:

The LORD is my strength and my defence;
he has become my salvation.
He is my God, and I will praise him,
my father's God, and I will exalt him.

(verse 2)

Gratitude inspires confidence – the God who brought them out of Egypt is the God who will bring them in to the Promised Land:

You will bring them in and plant them
on the mountain of your inheritance –
the place, LORD, you made for your dwelling,
the sanctuary, Lord, your hands established.

'The LORD reigns
for ever and ever.'

(verses 17–18)

We have experienced an even greater salvation. Whatever our circumstances, this never changes! There is no condemnation for those who are in Christ (Romans 8:1). We know that God works all things for our good in order to make us like Jesus (Romans 8:28–30). Nothing will ever separate us from the love of God poured into our lives by God (Romans 8:31–39).

These great blessings are secured on the basis of historical facts. Christ has died; Christ is risen; Christ is coming again. I remember hearing the testimony of Elisabeth Elliot, the widow of the martyred Jim Elliot. At her lowest ebb, she would read through the words of the Apostles' Creed. She explained that using these words challenged the darkness she was experiencing: *'However I feel, these things are true. They cannot change. I am secure in the love of the God who has broken into history and saved me.'*

Here is the foundation for a life of ceaseless gratitude. No matter what our circumstances are, the gospel always gives us a reason to be thankful.

The throne is occupied

Secondly, we are reminded that the living God is the God who rules:

> *He rules for ever by his power,*
> > *his eyes watch the nations –*
> > *let not the rebellious rise up against him.*
>
> > > > *(Psalm 66:7)*

God demonstrated his sovereign power when he crushed the forces of Egypt and the pantheon of gods that stood behind them. The horse and rider were thrown into the sea:

> The enemy boasted,
>> 'I will pursue, I will overtake them.
> I will divide the spoils;
>> I will gorge myself on them.
> I will draw my sword
>> and my hand will destroy them.'
> But you blew with your breath,
>> and the sea covered them.
> They sank like lead
>> in the mighty waters.
>
> *(Exodus 15:9–10)*

The psalmist rejoices in the comfort that this knowledge brings. Look at the four ways in which he describes the reign of God in verse 7.

God reigns permanently – *'he rules for ever'*. The events of time are planned in the mind of the eternal God. The whole of created history is but a fleeting episode in God's eternity. It is no wonder that we sometimes struggle with God's timing – you cannot hold an hourglass to the Creator of time.

He reigns independently – *'by his power'*. God does not have to ask permission. He is never taken by surprise. Nothing gets under his radar to trouble his plans. We may not understand what he wills, but we know that it is for our good.

He reigns intelligently – *'his eyes watch the nations'*. God knows everything that is happening from the fall of a leaf to the birth of the black hole. He knows the fine details of our lives. Our way is never hidden from the Lord.

And he reigns invincibly – *'let not the rebellious rise up against him'*. The rebellious nations can never overthrow God's rule. This is an immense comfort and source of joy to the Christian. We know that in all the circumstances of life, we are in God's hands. His plans towards us are always motivated by a benevolent and compassionate heart.

If God is in control, we can give thanks in all circumstances. Even the darkest providences cannot crush the heart that has discovered the grace of gratitude. Like Job we can say,

Naked I came from my mother's womb,
and naked I shall depart.
*The L*ORD *gave and the L*ORD *has taken away;*
*may the name of the L*ORD *be praised.*

(Job 1:21)

Reflections

1. Read the great hymn recorded in Exodus 15:1–18. What does it teach us about God? How should it help us to express the grace of gratitude?

2. Read Romans 8 and make a list of reasons why we should always be grateful to God.

3. How does the sovereignty of God cause our hearts to be grateful?

4

When gratitude is tested

Through the desert

In the next section of Psalm 66 the psalmist continues to reflect on the history of God's dealings with his people. He begins by remembering God's faithfulness:

> *Praise our God, all peoples,*
> > *let the sound of his praise be heard;*
> *he has preserved our lives*
> > *and kept our feet from slipping.*
>
> > (verses 8–9)

This section was probably inspired by the memories of Israel's experiences in the Wilderness. During those forty years Israel often strayed because of their ingratitude and a reckless determination to forget God's generosity. But he was always faithful. He preserved their lives (verse 9). Without God they would have ceased to exist.

God fed as many as two million people in a desert with the manna from heaven. He gave them water to drink (Exodus 17:1–7). As a child I had a picture Bible in which there was an illustration of Moses striking the rock and the water trickling out. And it was only a trickle. It did not hit me at the time, but imagine the amount of water needed to quench the thirst of two million people! In reality it must have looked like something out of *The Dam Busters*. God led them and protected them and was gracious to them in the midst of their constant rebelliousness.

This is the God who protects and provides for us today. As he is our God, then we will never be faced with a situation in which his resources will run dry. Peace is the conscious possession of adequate resources.

So, does that mean that the road to heaven will be pain free? Read on!

When tests come

The next part of Psalm 66 engages with some of the darker experiences of the desert:

> *For you, God, tested us;*
> *you refined us like silver.*
> *You brought us into prison*
> *and laid burdens on our backs.*
> *You let people ride over our heads;*
> *we went through fire and water,*
> *but you brought us to a place of abundance.*
> *(verses 10–12)*

The psalmist uses a series of metaphors to picture the severity of these trials. Think of a dark dungeon where hope is extinguished or imagine being crushed by burdens too heavy to bear. Picture a person lying on the ground under the hooves of a cavalry charge or imagine being incinerated in an all-consuming furnace with no apparent hope of escape or drowning under the floods of despair.

The metaphors are supposed to be evocative because life sometimes feels like this. The only condition for suffering is to live long enough. Can we really maintain a grateful heart in the middle of the furnace or under the pounding hooves of hardship?

We need to be clear here. Look at Romans 8:28: *'And we know that in all things God works for the good of those who love him, who have been called according to his purpose.'* Are *'all things'* good in themselves? Should I thank God for bereavement or persecution or a cot death or depression? Should I even thank God for sin? This would be bizarre and dehumanising. It stems from a misreading of the text. What is good is not *'all things'*, but the purposes of God. We rejoice in the purposes of God, not necessarily in the means that he uses. I can hate cancer and do everything in my power to overcome it, while at the same time trusting God and rejoicing that he is using even something as obscene as cancer to bring about his perfect purposes in my life.

My wife has struggled with multiple sclerosis for twenty-seven years. It has often been accompanied by pain that has robbed her of sleep and clouded her days. I hate multiple sclerosis. I hate what it has done to my beautiful wife. But together we have come to rejoice in the purposes of God and to see his hand in the midst of these trials. With good humour and God-given strength we can sing a song of gratitude in the storm.

Singing in the storm

Psalm 66 give us three reasons why we can sing during testing times.

Firstly, the psalmist reminds us that we are in the hands of God: 'For you, God, tested us' (verse 10). He has already asserted that the Lord rules over all things by his power (verse 7). Now he affirms that this includes the trials of life. It is God who tests us. The sovereignty of God is the soft pillow on which we rest our heads when life overwhelms us. Think of how God tested Abraham:

> Then God said, 'Take your son, your only son, whom you love – Isaac – and go to the region of Moriah. Sacrifice him there as a burnt offering on a mountain that I will show you' (Genesis 22:2).

It is difficult to imagine a more excruciating test. Not only does it wring the old man's heart, it also appears to put in jeopardy God's promise to bring salvation through Abraham's offspring. God seems to be acting out of character. It is easy for us to see the test from the other side, but Abraham did not know the outcome. How did he respond?

Early the next morning Abraham got up and loaded his donkey. He took with him two of his servants and his son Isaac. When he had cut enough wood for the burnt offering, he set out for the place God had told him about (Genesis 22:3).

Hebrews tells us that Abraham trusted that God would raise his son from the dead and so fulfil his purposes (Hebrews 11:17–19). He reasoned from what he already knew of God's character and this inspired and strengthened his faith. He knew that he was in God's hands and that God is all wise and does not make mistakes.

Refined like silver

This leads us to the psalmist's second aid to gratitude during hardships; God has a purpose in the test: *'you refined us like silver'* (Psalm 66:10).

Tests are not sent to destroy us but to perfect us. God means us good. A lump of rock is of little value, but imagine that I discover a sliver of silver in it. What do I do? I crush it and put it into a furnace in order to remove the dross and to produce the silver. This is what God is doing when he tests us:

> *For those God foreknew he also predestined to be conformed to the image of his Son, that he might be the firstborn among many brothers and sisters (Romans 8:29).*

God wants to make us like Jesus. Sometimes the furnace will have to be very hot indeed for him to achieve his desired goal. Yet we can lift up our eyes and look beyond the flames to see the smiling face of the one who loves us and is determined to make us like his Son.

How do we then respond? James tells us:

Consider it pure joy, my brothers and sisters, whenever you face trials of many kinds, because you know that the testing of your faith produces perseverance. Let perseverance finish its work so that you may be mature and complete, not lacking anything (James 1:2–4).

My first job was teaching RE in a large comprehensive school in Wiltshire. The GCSE course involved the study of Luke's gospel. The pupils had to answer forty multiple-choice questions based on Luke. My best pupil, Jackie, scored a perfect score in her mock exam. She was a lovely Christian girl who worked very hard at her studies. I was invigilating in the real exam and happened to look over Jackie's shoulder and notice she had missed out the first question, which meant that the sequence was disrupted. All her answers were right, but they were in the wrong order. She would score no marks. I was not allowed to say anything, but for the next fifty minutes I willed her to check her work and to make the slight adjustment that was needed. With five minutes to go she discovered her mistake and asked for another answer paper so that she could correct it. She quickly ran down the page, transferring the crosses to the new paper. As the exam ended, she completed the task. She passed with flying colours!

When God tests us, he is always close and he is always willing us to pass. We can trust him completely.

Home at last

Thirdly, and finally, the psalmist tells us that we can sing in the storm because we know that one day it will end: *'but you brought us to a place of abundance'* (Psalm 66:12).

The Wilderness was a place of testing for Israel. They often reacted badly to the tests and responded with grumbling instead of gratitude. Nonetheless, God was faithful and brought them into the Promised Land – *'a place of abundance'*.

In our lives tests seem intolerable because they feel interminable. This can be true of chronic illness or a dysfunctional relationship or the numbness of bereavement. But every trial will one day end. God has promised to bring us into a place of abundance. Peter describes it as an inheritance that does not perish, spoil or fade and is secure:

> *This inheritance is kept in heaven for you, who through faith are shielded by God's power until the coming of the salvation that is ready to be revealed in the last time (1 Peter 1:4-5).*

As we fix our eyes on our inheritance, we can look beyond the test and rejoice that the best is yet to be:

> *In all this you greatly rejoice, though now for a little while you may have had to suffer grief in all kinds of trials (1 Peter 1:6).*

It may not seem like a *'little while'*, but in the light of eternity it will soon be over. One day we will be home and all tears will be gone for ever.

Guard your heart

Armed with these biblical insights, we can turn groaning and grumbling into gratitude and gratefulness. But one final warning needs to be sounded. God tested Israel in the Wilderness to discover what was in their hearts:

> *Remember how the LORD your God led you all the way in the wilderness these forty years, to humble and test you in order to know what was in your heart, whether or not you would keep his commands (Deuteronomy 8:2).*

By their actions they often revealed that their hearts were full of unbelief and disobedience. We glibly say that tests are good for us. That is only true if we respond with humble faith and trust in our Father, knowing that he is acting in love and wisdom. The trial that makes one person better can make another bitter.

Guard your heart.

Reflections

1. In what ways does God test us? How is he testing you at the moment?

2. God has a purpose in the tests he sends into our lives. What do these verses

teach us about some of God's purposes:
Romans 5:1–5; 2 Corinthians 1:3–11;
12:5–10; Hebrews 12:1–13;
1 Peter 4:12–16?

3. In 2 Corinthians 4:17 Paul tells us to
   compare our current trials with the
   glory to come (see also Romans 8:18).
   How can we do this?

5

The triumph
of gratitude

Laying at God's feet

At this point in Psalm 66 we move from global invitation and national proclamation to personal affirmation (verses 13–20).

> *Come and hear, all you who fear God;*
> *let me tell you what he has done for me.*
>
> *(verse 16)*

It is this section which persuades many commentators that this is indeed the psalm of Hezekiah. It speaks of a glorious deliverance at the hands of God and the gratitude that flows from this.

Remember the story. Surrounded by the Assyrians, Jerusalem's situation looked hopeless. The commander of this invincible army sent a letter to Hezekiah warning him not to trust God (2 Kings 19:10–11). The letter dripped with contempt for God and malicious intent towards his people.

We live in a world that is often utterly contemptuous to our God and his gospel. It mocks our confidence in him and suggests that we are deluded. What do you do when you get bad news that seems to undermine your trust in God? Hezekiah knew exactly what to do:

Hezekiah received the letter from the messengers and read it. Then he went up to the temple of the LORD and spread it out before the LORD (2 Kings 19:14).

What a wonderful picture of prayer! Prayer is simply laying out our circumstances at the feet of God. Prayer is telling God what he already knows, but with a sigh from the heart and a cry for help. So we could pray:

> *This is too much for me, Lord. I don't know how to deal with it. But I know who you are and I place it in your hands. Please act on my behalf because I cannot defend myself.*

God's answer came in less than twenty-four hours and the Assyrian army was obliterated (2 Kings 19:35–36). The good reasons for believing that Psalm 66 was written in response to this deliverance are that Hezekiah records his response (verses 13–15) and shares his testimony (verses 16-20).

Consecration

How do you respond to a great deliverance?

> *I will come to your temple with burnt offerings*
>   *and fulfil my vows to you –*
> *vows my lips promised and my mouth spoke*
>   *when I was in trouble.*
> *I will sacrifice fat animals to you*

and an offering of rams;
I will offer bulls and goats.

(verses 13–15)

In his time of trouble Hezekiah had turned to God and cried for help. He appears to have made certain vows to the Lord. We need to be careful here. The Bible does not teach that we can barter or bargain with God. We do not buy his blessing with the promise of sacrifice. His generosity flows from his heart of grace.

So, what does Hezekiah mean? I think he is telling us that in his heart he determined that when God rescued him, he would not forget it but would make much of it. He would celebrate God's goodness and give a public display of his gratitude. And this is exactly what he did. The Assyrians had threatened the very existence of the temple. He went into the temple and offered a plethora of sacrifices of thanksgiving.

There is clearly a warning here – forgetfulness leads to ingratitude. Isaiah, who ministered in Jerusalem during the Assyrian crisis, begins his ministry with a warning of the dangers of spiritual amnesia:

Hear me, you heavens! Listen, earth!
*For the L*ORD *has spoken:*
'I reared children and brought them up,
but they have rebelled against me.
The ox knows its master,
the donkey its owner's manger,
but Israel does not know,
my people do not understand.'

(Isaiah 1:2–3)

Shakespeare's King Lear, deserted and betrayed by two of his daughters, laments,

How sharper than a serpent's tooth it is
To have a thankless child![5]

The ingratitude of his daughters sends the king mad. It is like the bite of a venomous snake. Yet ingratitude was the common response of Israel during their long history. Hezekiah may have been thankful, but most of the kings and the majority of the people forgot God's kindnesses to them. Many of the problems in our lives or families or churches stem from a

---

[5.] William Shakespeare, *King Lear*, Act 1, Scene 4, lines 288–289.

failure to remember God's goodness. The road to joyful thanksgiving lies along the route of perpetual remembrance:

> *Praise the LORD, my soul;*
> *all my inmost being, praise his holy name.*
> *Praise the LORD, my soul,*
> *and forget not all his benefits*
>
> *(Psalm 103:1–2)*

A grateful heart will lead to a life of praise and issue in glad and joyful surrender to God and his purposes. Paul borrows the imagery of sacrifice to describe the life of holiness:

> *Follow God's example, therefore, as dearly loved children and live a life of love, just as Christ loved us and gave himself up for us as a fragrant offering and sacrifice to God (Ephesians 5:1–2).*

We offer not animal sacrifices, but ourselves as living sacrifices (Romans 12:1–2). This is the true expression of thanksgiving which is pleasing to God.

The holy God who hears

The second thing that Hezekiah does is to testify to God's goodness:

> Come and hear, all you who fear God;
>   let me tell you what he has done for me.
> I cried out to him with my mouth;
>   his praise was on my tongue.
> If I had cherished sin in my heart,
>   the Lord would not have listened;
> but God has surely listened
>   and has heard my prayer.
> Praise be to God,
>   who has not rejected my prayer
>   or withheld his love from me!
>
> (Psalm 66:16–20)

We call people to see what God has done (verse 5) – this is what we do every time we preach the gospel. But we can also invite them to hear what the Lord has done for us (verse 16). We have a story to tell and a testimony to share.

Hezekiah's testimony concerns answered prayer. He tells us that his prayer was simple and passionate: *'I cried out to him with my mouth'* (verse 17). God does not hear us because of the eloquence of our prayers or the elegance of our theology. He listens because we come to him through Jesus (Ephesians 2:18; Hebrews 10:19–22). We see this too in Matthew 6:7–8:

And when you pray, do not keep on babbling like pagans, for they think they will be heard because of their many words. Do not be like them, for your Father knows what you need before you ask him.

Hezekiah's petition was mixed with praise (Psalm 66:17). Likewise, Paul reminds us:

Rejoice always, pray continually, give thanks in all circumstances; for this is God's will for you in Christ Jesus (1 Thessalonians 5:16–18).

Praise lifts our minds above our circumstances and reminds us of God's glory and power.

But there is a sting in the tail. 'Cherished sin' will cut off our communication with God (Psalm 66:18). What does Hezekiah mean by this? He cannot mean sin in general. If God did not listen to the prayers of sinners, none of us would be heard.

We struggle with sin and we need forgiveness every day (Matthew 6:11–13; 1 John 1:9–10). Our assurance is based on Christ's finished work for us and our access is secured by his merits alone. So, Hezekiah cannot be saying that we need to wait till we are sinless before we can be assured that God will listen.

I think that cherished sin is something else. It refers to those sins that we love so much that we are unwilling to abandon them. God may put his finger on them when we turn to prayer, but we refuse to let go: 'I'll do anything but that, Lord. That belongs to me and you cannot have it.' Once we say that, God's ear is no longer open.

The obvious cherished sin which cuts off our communication with God is unforgiveness (Matthew 6:12–15; 18:21–35). But it may be a habit we treasure more than God; a relationship we prize more than his smile; a website which we relish even though we know that its effects are toxic.

The problem with these sins is that they become the furniture of our lives. We are no longer aware of their effects. A preacher once visited a farm. The farmer ploughed his field with a perfectly straight furrow, until he came to the centre of the field where there was an old stump. At this point he simply worked around the stump. The visitor remarked on this afterwards, to which the farmer replied, 'There used to be a tree there in my grandfather's time. It was struck by lightning. The stump has been there ever since. It was there in my father's time; I guess it will be there in my son's time.'

'I see,' replied his friend. 'But have you never thought of pulling the stump up?' It had never occurred to the farmer!

Sometimes we just get used to our cherished sins: 'It's always been there; it's just the way I am; I tried to deal with it once, but failed – what am I supposed to do?' Then we wonder why our fellowship with God is stilted and our spiritual growth is stunted. The love of sin leads to indifference and coldness towards God.

Are there any stumps in your life at the moment?

The psalmist gets up from his knees confident that there is no cherished sin to discover and with the assurance that God has been listening (Psalm 66:19). We can have the same certainty.

This great psalm of thanksgiving ends on a high note affirming God's love:

> *Praise be to God,*
> *who has not rejected my prayer*
> *or withheld his love from me!*

> *(verse 20)*

It is this unchanging love which is the strongest foundation for a life of gratitude. A thankful heart marks out a person who has been convinced that, amid all the vagaries of life, it is well with their soul and their relationship with God. Even in the toughest times I am buoyed up by his love. Grateful praise flows from this knowledge and is fortified by it.

Reflections

1. 'The road to joyful thanksgiving lies along the route of perpetual remembrance.' Read Psalm 103 and

make a list of all the things for which David is thankful.

2. What stops you praying? What have you learned from this psalm which might help you to pray more effectively?

3. Do you have any stumps in your life which need removing? What are you going to do about them?

Conclusion

Can you remember the thank-you letters to half-forgotten relatives that you had to write when you were children? 'Dear Auntie Matilda, thank you so much for the green hankie with red spots. I've always wanted one … but not much.' My kids used to refer to them as the dark side of Christmas.

Sometimes that's what gratitude feels like. But it shouldn't. Real gratitude sings on the darkest days and is stronger than anything that life can throw at it. Gratitude is a supernatural grace implanted in the hearts of God's children. We cannot create it, but we can sustain it. Psalm 66 has taught us some of the ways in which we can nurture this grace, living glad and grateful lives:

Gratitude is a choice – we cannot control our circumstances, but we can control our response.

Gratitude appreciates the good things that God has poured into our lives and deliberately affirms the goodness and worth of the Giver.

Gratitude is a deep-seated delight grounded in the unchanging and unshakable character of God.

Gratitude will express itself in song and is nourished by praise and adoration.

Gratitude is not subject to the swirling waters of human speculation but is firmly anchored on the rock of the saving deeds of the living God.

Gratitude delights in remembering all that God has done – forgetfulness leads to ingratitude.

Gratitude boasts in the gospel of God's grace in Christ – no matter what our circumstances are, the gospel always gives us a reason to be thankful.

Gratitude delights that God is in control of all circumstances and knows that God is working all things for our good.

Gratitude has its eyes on eternity.

Gratitude marks out a person who has been convinced that, amid all the vagaries of life, it is well with their soul and their relationship with God.

When we turn to the fuller revelation of the New Testament, we find this same spirit of gratitude marking out those who have come to know and love Jesus Christ.

So Paul, in prison and facing an uncertain future, can write,

> *I know what it is to be in need, and I know what it is to have plenty. I have learned the secret of being content in any and every situation, whether well fed or hungry, whether living in plenty or in want. I can do all this through him who gives me strength (Philippians 4:12–13).*

He had chosen gratitude.

So should we.

 Publishing

10Publishing is committed to publishing
quality Christian resources that are biblical,
accessible and point people to Jesus.

www.10ofthose.com is our online
retail partner selling thousands of
quality books at discounted prices.

For information contact: **info@10ofthose.com**
or check out our website: **www.10ofthose.com**